G000123646

Printed in the United States of America

First Printing, 2017

ISBN 9781973480624

2mm Publishing
www.amazon.com/author/2mmpublishing

Welcome to best 101 jokes about Donald Trump!

Warning!

The problem with these jokes are that Republicans don't think they're funny, and Democrats don't think they're jokes.

1. What do Donald Trump and an adult film star have in common?

   A. They are both experts at switching positions in front of a camera.

2. Why are Muslims also worried about Trumps immigration plans?

   A. Once you deport Juan you deport Jamal.

3. What is Donald Trump's favorite type of clothing?

   A. Russian ties.

4. What does the Trump administration use instead of emails?

   A. Alternative fax.

5. Say what you like about Donald Trump...

   A. But he is doing more than anyone else in the world to get the US President impeached.

6. If Donald Trump becomes President I'm going to Mexico.

   A. Not by choice though.

7. The 2016 US Presidential Election.

   A. That's it. That's the entire fucking joke.

8. What does Donald Trump's wife call it when he takes Viagra?

   A. A rigged erection

9. What do Donald Trump and his father have in common?

    A. They both have shitty judgment when it comes to pulling out.

10. Steve Jobs would've been a better president than Trump...

    A. But I guess comparing apples to oranges is unfair.

11. A Mexican kid meets Donald Trump and says to him, "I want to be President one day."

Trump says, "Are you stupid? Are you an idiot? Out of your mind? Are you retarded?"

The kid replies, "You know what, I've changed my mind. Those are too many requirements."

12. Why will the congress never impeach Trump?

    A. Because the republicans always insist on carrying a baby to full term.

13. Bill Gates has agreed to pay for Trump's wall...

    A. On the condition he gets to install windows.

14. Liberals are acting like Trump is going to kill all the gays, make slavery legal again, and take away women's rights....

    A. Like he's a Muslim or something.

15. How much is Donald Trump's life insurance?

    A. Just one pence.

16. Why does Trump wear a tie?

   A. If he takes it off, the foreskin flies up over his head.

17. Looks like Trump is keeping up Michelle's ideals of getting America fit again...

   A. One day in office and he has thousands of people getting up and going out for walks on this beautiful Saturday morning.

18. If Trump is elected president...

   A. He will be the first billionaire to move into government housing after a black man.

19. What do Donald Trump & the iPhone 7 have in common?

   A. They both think de-porting is the answer when there's no more Jobs.

20. President Donald Trump and his driver were cruising along a country road one night when all of a sudden they hit a pig, killing it instantly.

Trump told his driver to go up to the farmhouse and explain to the owners what had happened. About one hour later Trump sees his driver staggering back to the car with a bottle of wine in one hand, a cigar in the other and his clothes all ripped and torn.

"What happened to you?" asked Trump

"Well, the Farmer gave me the wine, his wife gave me the cigar and his 19-year-old daughter made mad passionate love to me."

"My God, what did you tell them?" asks Trump.

The driver replies, "I'm President Donald Trump's driver, and I just killed the pig."

21. What's the difference between a Trump and a flying pig?

A. The letter F

22. The Pope and Trump are on stage in front of a huge crowd.

The Pope leaned towards Mr. Trump and said, "Do you know that with one little wave of my hand I can make every person in this crowd go wild with joy? This joy will not be a momentary display, like that of your followers, but go deep into their hearts and for the rest of their lives whenever they speak of this day, they will rejoice!"

Trump replied, "I seriously doubt that. With one little wave of your hand? Show me!"

So the Pope slapped him

23. When Trump borrows $1,000,000 from his dad it's a small loan...

   A. But when he donates that much money to Texas, it's a yuuuge contribution

24. Trump said in his campaign that if I voted for Clinton, I would be stuck with a criminal president under constant federal investigation from day one...

    A. Turns out, he was right. I voted for Clinton and I'm stuck with a criminal president under federal investigation from day one.

25. So Barack Obama and Donald Trump somehow ended up at the same barber shop. As they sat there, each being worked on by a different barber, not a word was spoken. The barbers were both afraid to start a conversation, for fear that it would turn nasty. As the barbers finished their shaves in silence, the one who had Trump in his chair reached for the aftershave.

But Donald was quick to stop him, jokingly saying, "No thanks. My wife, Melania, will smell that and think I've been in a brothel."

The second barber turned to Barack and said, "How about you, Mr. Obama ?"

Barack replied, "Go right ahead, my wife Michelle doesn't know what the inside of a brothel smells like."

26. Republicans are the true snowflakes...

    A. They're white, they're cold, and if you put enough of them together they'll shut down public schools

27. Donald Trump: "I'm not orange!"

    A. "Impeach."

28. Donald Trump has decided to take just $1 as his salary for the job of the President instead of the usual $400,000...

    A. That man would do just about anything to avoid paying the taxes.

29. Did you hear that NYC paid Hillary Clinton $2,000,000 as a consultant for New Years Eve?

    A. They wanted an expert on dropping the ball at the last second.

30. Trump's wall will cost $21.6 billion, Nasa's budget is only $19 billion...

    A. Probably because Mexico has more aliens

31. There's a term for Presidents like Trump...

    A. Probably not two terms, though.

32. Donald Trump steps out onto the White House lawn in the dead of winter. Right in front of him, on the White House lawn, he sees "Donald Trump Sucks" written in urine across the snow.

    Well, he's is pretty ticked off. He storms into his security staff's HQ, and yells "Somebody wrote an insult in the snow on the front damn lawn! And they wrote it in urine! Whoever did it had to be standing right on the porch when he did it! Where were you guys?!" The security guys stay silent and stare ashamedly at the floor.

    Trump hollers "Well dammit, don't just sit there! Get out and find out who did it! I want an answer, and I want it tonight!"

The entire staff immediately jump up and race for the exits.

Later that evening, his chief security officer approaches him and says: "Well Mr. President, we have some bad news and we have some really bad news. Which do you want first?"

Trump says "Give me the bad news first."

The officer says "Well, we took a sample of the urine and tested it. The results just came back, and it was Mike Pence's urine."

Trump says "Oh my god, I feel so... so... betrayed! My own vice president! Damn. ...Well, what's the really bad news?"

The officer replies "Well, it's Melania's handwriting."

33. Donald Trump dies and goes to Hell. Satan is already waiting for him.

"Well, I don't know what to do. See, you're on my list, but I have no free rooms for you. But you, you definitely have to stay in hell, so I'll have to find a solution. There are a few people here who aren't as bad as you are... I guess I'll let one go and you'll take their place. However, you can choose whose place you want to take." Satan explains.

"Oh, that sounds okay I guess" says Trump.

Satan leads him to the first room and opens the door. In this room, there's a huge swimming pool. In it, Reagan is drowning. He goes down, then up, then down, then up, and he's gasping for air all the while.

"Oh, no," says Trump. "That's not for me, I'm a poor swimmer."

Satan opens the second door. The room is full of rocks and they see Nixon trying to break up the rocks with a wooden hammer.

"Nah, I have problems with my shoulders and my back, that'd be such a painful thing to do day after day."

So Satan opens the third door. In the room, they see Bill Clinton lying on the floor, all tied up. Monica Lewinsky is lying on top of Clinton, giving him a blowjob.

Trump stares at the scene with a wide smile and say, "Ah, that I could endure!"

"Alright," laughs Satan. "Monica, you're free to go!"

34. In breaking news, Trump's personal library has burned down...

    A. The fire consumed both books and in a tragic twist he hadn't even finished coloring the second one

35. I don't normally see eye to eye with most Trump supporters, but if there's one thing we do agree on...

    A. It's that the president of Puerto Rico is the dumbest son of a bitch to ever hold public office.

36. Not everything Donald Trump says is stupid.

    A. The Chinese built a wall 2,000 years ago - and they still don't have any Mexicans!

37. It's going to be easy for Trump to build that wall...

    A. Everyone's shitting bricks everywhere!

38. Why does Donald Trump take Xanax?

    A. For Hispanic attacks.

39. Donald Trump has labelled Hillary Clinton "disgusting" for taking a bathroom break during the debate...

    A. Trump himself never has to go to the bathroom, as the shit just comes straight out of his mouth.

40. I don't support Trump, but I would never denigrate his supporters

    A. If you're a Trump supporter, "denigrate" means "to put down."

41. After a long life, and a tumultuous presidency, Donald J Trump dies and arrives at the Gates of Heaven, where he sees a huge wall of clocks behind him.

He asks an angel, "What are all those clocks?"

The angel answers, "Those are Lie-Clocks. Everyone on Earth has a Lie-Clock. Every time you lie the hands on your clock will move."

"Oh," says Trump, "whose clock is that?"

"That's Washington's clock. The hands have never moved, indicating that he never told a lie."

"Tremendous" says Trump. "And whose clock is that one?"

The angel responds, "That's Abraham Lincoln's clock. The hands have moved twice, telling us that Abe told only two lies in his entire life."

"So, where's my clock?" Asks Trump

"Oh, your clock is in God's office. He's using it as a ceiling fan."

42. John (while writing Revelations): "So Lord, the end will be signaled by trumpets?"

God: "No... I said Trump/Pence."

43. Donald Trump was asked if he could quote any Bible verses...

   A. He replied,"Give a man a fish and he will eat for a day. Deport him and you do not have to feed him again." - Trump 20:16

44. A swastika has been spray painted over Donald Trump's star on the Hollywood Walk of Fame...

   A. Police say it's impossible to tell if the act was committed by Trump's opponents or supporters.

45. Trump: The less immigrants that come in, the better

    Pence: The fewer

    Trump: I told you not to call me that yet

46. Donald Trump is visiting a elementary school and he visits one of the classes. They are in the middle of a discussion related to words and their meanings. The teacher asks Mr. Trump if he would like to lead the discussion of the word "tragedy." So he asks the class for an example of a tragedy.

    One little boy stands up and offers, "If my best friend who lives on a farm, is playing in the field and a runaway tractor comes along and knocks him dead, that would be a tragedy."

    "No," says Mr Trump, "that would be an accident."

    A little girl raises her hand, "If a school bus carrying 50 children drove over a cliff, killing everyone inside, that would be a tragedy."

    "I'm afraid not," explains the exalted businessman. "That's what we would call a great loss."

    The room goes silent. No other children volunteer.

Mr. Trump searches the room. "Isn't there someone here who can give me an example of a tragedy?"

Finally at the back of the room, little Johnny raises his hand.

In a quiet voice he says, "If a private jet carrying you was struck by a missile and blown to smithereens, that would be a tragedy."

"Fantastic!" exclaims Mr. Trump, "That's right. And can you tell me why that would be a tragedy?"

"Well," says the boy, "because it sure as hell wouldn't be a great loss and it probably wouldn't be an accident either."

47. Donald Trump goes to a fortune teller and asks "When am I going to die?"

The fortune teller replies,"you will die on a major Mexican holiday."

Trump asks, "Which Mexican holiday? Cinco de Mayo? Dia de los muertos?"

The fortune teller replies, "ANY day you die, Donald, will be a major Mexican holiday!"

48. A plane with Jeb Bush, Donald Trump, Hillary Clinton & Bernie Sanders is about to crash, but has only 3 parachutes.

The first passenger yells, "I'm Jeb Bush, let the big dog eat! I can't afford to die."

He took the first parachute and jumped.

The second passenger, Donald Trump, runs screaming, "I'm the smartest man in the world & the next President of America."

He grabbed the second parachute and jumped.

The third passenger, Hillary Clinton, says to Bernie Sanders, "take the last parachute."

Bernie says, "It's ok Hillary, there is a parachute for both of us. The world's smartest man just took my backpack."

49. Trump wants to ban the sale of pre-shredded cheese.

    A. He wants to make America grate again.

50. A lone sniper was just about to assassinate Donald Trump. Just at the last moment, one of the President's bodyguards spotted him.

He immediately shouted "Mickey Mouse, Mickey Mouse."

A shot rang out and Trump fell dead.

As his aides gathered round the body, one of them asked the bodyguard why he had shouted "Mickey Mouse"

"I'm sorry" he said "I meant to shout "Donald, duck"

51. On the night of his inauguration, Donald Trump is visited by 3 ghosts. Early in the night, FDR appears.

Trump asks him "how can I make America great again?"

FDR replies "think only of the people; do not make laws based on hatred, bigotry, or with the thought of lining your own pockets"

Trump's face sours, "FAKE NEWS!" he screams and FDR disappears.

Trump falls back to sleep. A few hours later, he is awakened by George Washington's ghost.

Trump asks, "how can I make America great again?"

Washington replies, "I would suggest you never tell a lie", which infuriates Trump.

Trump screams for his bodyguards but Washington is already gone. Around 3 in the morning, he is visited by the ghost of Abraham Lincoln.

Again, he asks "how can I make America great again?"

Lincoln thinks for a bit and says "go to the theater."

52. While stitching a cut on the hand of a 75 year old farmer, the doctor struck up a conversation with the old man. Eventually the topic got around to Donald Trump and his role as the Republican Nominee for President.

The old farmer said, " Well, as I see it, Donald Trump is like a 'Post Tortoise'."

Not being familiar with the term, the doctor asked him what a 'post tortoise' was.

The old farmer said, "When you're driving down a country road and you come across a fence post with a tortoise balanced on top, that's a post tortoise."

The old farmer saw the puzzled look on the doctor's face so he continued to explain.

"You know he didn't get up there by himself, he doesn't belong up there, he doesn't know what to do while he's up there, he's elevated beyond his ability to function, and you just wonder what kind of dumb ass put him up there to begin with."

53. A teacher asked her 6th grade class how many of them were Trump fans.

Not really knowing what a Trump fan is, but wanting to be liked by their teacher, all the kids raised their hands except for Little Johnny.

The teacher asked Little Johnny why he has decided to be different... again. Little Johnny said, "Because I'm not a Trump fan."

The teacher asked, "Why aren't you a fan of Trump?"

Johnny said, "Because I'm a Democrat."

The teacher asked him why he's a Democrat.

Little Johnny answered, "Well, my Mom's a Democrat and my Dad's a Democrat, so I'm a Democrat."

Annoyed by this answer, the teacher asked, "If your mom was a moron and your dad was an idiot, what would that make you?"

With a big smile, Little Johnny replied, "A Trump fan."

54. Donald Trump gets executed and is hanged by the neck until dead. At Trump Tower, his family watches CNN, which is covering his death live, all of them mournful and teary before Donald himself walks in triumphantly.

"But Donald, CNN says you were killed!" Ivanka cried.

"Nope!" Donnie beamed, holding up the rope that was used to hang him, "fake noose."

55. The Pentagon is changing the nuclear codes to over 140 characters

    A. So Trump can't Tweet it.

56. What is the difference between Russia and reality?

    A. Trump had connections with Russia

57. If Hillary Clinton and Donald Trump are in a boat and it capsizes. Who survives?

    A. America

58. Obama and Trump are running laps around the White House, after three laps Trump excitedly yells "10 minutes exactly, well that has to be a new record!".

Obama says "I don't think so, Bush did 9:11".

59. The US Postal Services releases a stamp with a picture of President Trump. But the new stamp was not sticking to envelopes. This enraged the President, who demanded a full investigation.

After weeks of testing and $1.73 million in congressional spending, a special Presidential commission presented the following findings:

The stamp is in perfect order. There is nothing wrong with the adhesive. The fact is, people are spitting on the wrong side.

60. How's Donald Trump going to get rid of all the Mexicans?

A. Juan by Juan

61. Why did Donald Trump secretly want to lose the election?

A. Because by winning, he'll have to move into a smaller house in a black neighborhood.

62. George Bush, Barack Obama and Donald Trump are going for a job interview with God.

God asks Bush: "What do you believe in?"

Bush replies: "I believe in a free economy, a strong America, the American nation and so on ..."

God is impressed by Bush and tells him: "Great, come sit on the chair on my right."

God goes to Obama and asks: "What do you believe in?"

Obama replies: "I believe in democracy, helping the poor, world peace, etc. ..."

God is really impressed by Obama and tells him: "Well done, come sit on the chair on my left."

Finally, God asks Trump: "What do you believe in"?

Trump replies: "I believe you're sitting on my chair."

63. Why is Trump so keen to build a wall to keep out Mexican rapists?

    A. He's afraid of the competition.

64. Donald Trump is flying over New York City.

He looks out of the window and says to his family, "You know what, I'm gonna throw ten $100 bills out of the window and make ten people very happy!"

His son looks at him and says, "Dad, why don't you throw two hundred $5 bills out of the window? Then you can make two hundred people happy."

Donald says, "Son, that's a great idea!"

His wife turns to him and says, "Donald, why not throw one thousand $1 bills out the window? You could make one thousand people happy!"

Donald looks at her and says, "Babe, that is a fantastic idea! The best I've heard!"

The pilot turns and looks at Trump and says, "As long as you're at it, why don't you throw yourself out of the window and make millions of people happy?"

65. What's 18 inches long and hangs in front of an asshole?

A. Donald Trump's tie.

66. To be fair, Donald Trump HAS created a lot of jobs...

    A. It's going to take a lot of people to clean up this mess.

67. Minorities have the race card, women have the gender card, homosexuals have the gay card, but what do discriminatory white men have?

    A. A Trump card.

68. What happens when Donald Trump takes Viagra?

    A. He grows taller

69. America is going to suffer if Donald Trump becomes president.

    A. You could say they are going toupee for it.

70. What do a thong and Donald Trump's toupee have in common?

    A. They both cover an asshole.

71. Why did Donald Trump marry an immigrant?

    A. Once again, immigrants are doing the jobs no American want to do.

72. What do Donald Trump and a pumpkin have in common?

    A. They're orange on the outside, hollow on the inside and should be tossed out in early November.

73. I wish I had Trump as a teacher...

    A. Citations would be easy

    "You know it, I know it, everyone knows it"

74. I'm sick of people comparing Trump to Hitler.

    A. Hitler wrote his own book.

75. People keep grouping all Trump supporters with these Nazi movements recently, which I disagree with and think is quite silly...

    A. After all, the Russians fought against the Nazis.

76. A guy looking for a fight walks into a biker bar and shouts, "Donald Trump is an asshole."

The biggest guys in the bar gets in his face and warns him, "You better watch what you say around here."

"Why? Are you a Trump supporter?"

"No, I'm an asshole."

77. After too much effort during a state visit in Israel, Trump collapses of a heart attack.

The Israeli officials take the body and tell the Americans, "There's two options. The first one, you pay $5,000,000 and we send the body back to the United States so he can be buried there. Second option, you pay $100,000 and we bury him here in the sacred land of Israel"

After much debating, the Americans decided to pay the larger fee and repatriate the body. Surprised, the Israelis ask them why they chose the bigger figure.

"Well, the last time you buried someone he came back after three days so we're not taking any chances!"

78. What is the only reason Donald Trump is watching the Olympics?

    A. So he can determine how high Mexican pole vaulters can jump.

79. If Donald Trump wants to destroy North Korea...

    A. Perhaps he should move there and become their leader.

80. What is Donald Trump's favorite nation?

    A. Discrimination

81. Why don't Melania and Donald Trump sleep in the same bed?

    A. She was tired of Putin's snoring.

82. Trump has two parts of brain, 'left' and 'right'...

    A. In the left side, there's nothing right. In the right side, there's nothing left.

83. Donald Trump and Hillary Clinton walk into a bakery. As soon as they enter the bakery, Hillary steals three pastries and puts them in her pocket.

She says to Donald, "See how clever I am? The owner didn't see anything and I don't even need to lie."

Donald says to Hillary, "That's the typical dishonesty you have displayed throughout your entire life, trickery and deceit. I am going to show you an honest way to get the same result."

Trump goes to the owner of the bakery and says, "Give me a pastry and I will show you a magic trick."

Intrigued, the owner accepts and gives him a pastry. Trump swallows it and asks for another one. The owner gives him another one. Then Trump asks for a third pastry and eats that, too.

The owner is starting to wonder where the magic trick is and asks, "What did you do with the pastries?"

Trump replies, "Look in Hillary's pocket!"

84. How is Trump's Presidency like climate change?

    A. Every day it gets worse and Republicans try to deny it.

85. A man notices a Mexican bookstore. He decides to go in because he has never seen a Mexican book store before.

He browses through the store and finally asks the clerk, "Do you have the book on Donald Trump's foreign policies with Mexico?"

The clerk replies, "Fuck you!! Get out, and stay out!!"

The man replies, "Yeah, that's the one!"

86. Do you know what Mexicans think about Trump's wall?

    A. Who cares? They'll get over it.

87. Donald Trump is like top shelf vodka

    A. Expensive, Transparent, and wouldn't be here if not for Russia.

88. Donald Trump truly made history...

    A. Winning an argument against a woman.

89. Why don't you want to play Uno with Donald Trump?

    A. He takes away all the green cards.

90. Donald Trump walks into a bar...

    A. And lowers it.

91. Trump is going too far...

    A. He deported a printer because it didn't have papers.

92. Kim Jong Un and Putin were fighting about who was going to put people on Mars first.

Trump steps in and says, "That doesn't matter America is going to land on the sun first".

The Russian and North Korean said "you can't land on the sun it's too hot and you will die."

Trump responded, "Ha! You idiots! America is going to land there at night."

93. What does Melania see in Donald Trump?

    A. Ten billion dollars and high cholesterol!

94. What is Donald Trump's favorite chewing gum?

    A. Bigly Chew

95. What is the name of Donald Trump's new private jet?

    A. Hair Force One.

96. Why does Trump love the poorly educated?

    A. Because they only know their ABC's: "Anybody But Clinton".

97. Why don't black cats cross Trump's path?

    A. Because they are afraid of pussy grabbers.

98. A white man, a black man and an orange man walk into the bar.

The white man goes up to the bar to order a whiskey.

The barman goes, "Hey, aren't you George Bush?"

"Yes, I am" he replies.

"Well Mr. President it's an honor."

Then the black man goes up to the bar to get his drink.

"Hey, aren't you Barack Obama?" asks the barman.

"Yes I am", Obama responds.

"Two presidents in my bar in one day; this is the highlight of my life" the barman gushes.

Then the orange man walks up to the bar. The barman immediately tells him to get out of the bar.

Furiously, the orange man asks why and the barman exclaims "Ted; you just got a new liver last week. Your wife would kill me if I gave you a drink."

99. How do you know you're reading one of Donald
    Trump's books?

    A. It starts on Chapter 11.

100.   What do Donald Trump, Dale Earnhardt &
Pink Floyd have in common?

    A. The Wall!

101.   Why does the Donald sleep with a potato in
his briefs?

    A. Because he want to wake up some day as
America's First Dictator.

18554100R00023

Printed in Great Britain
by Amazon